T0148003

The
Mommy
Rule
Book

The Mommy Rule Book

JOHANNA REDEYE

(PAY ATTENTION!!)

authorHOUSE®

AuthorHouse™
1663 Liberty Drive
Bloomington, IN 47403
www.authorhouse.com
Phone: 1-800-839-8640

© 2011 by Johanna Redeye. All rights reserved.

No part of this book may be reproduced, stored in a retrieval system, or transmitted by any means without the written permission of the author.

First published by AuthorHouse   11/12/2011

ISBN: 978-1-4685-0043-1 (sc)
ISBN: 978-1-4685-0044-8 (ebk)

Library of Congress Control Number: 2011960214

Printed in the United States of America

Any people depicted in stock imagery provided by Thinkstock are models, and such images are being used for illustrative purposes only.
Certain stock imagery © Thinkstock.

This book is printed on acid-free paper.

Because of the dynamic nature of the Internet, any web addresses or links contained in this book may have changed since publication and may no longer be valid. The views expressed in this work are solely those of the author and do not necessarily reflect the views of the publisher, and the publisher hereby disclaims any responsibility for them.

To the children of my family and the children of my heart:

All mothers hope they have prepared their children for the challenges of life. Decades of life experiences (some fun, some not so fun) and the wisdom of generations of mothers have shaped my outlook and given me direction. However, just in case you didn't hear them the first time or have forgotten all the "reminders" over the years, here they are again.

I love you lots.

People don't do things *to* you; they do them *for* themselves.

I am less important than I believe! How often have I had the mistaken idea that some slight or annoying act was directed wholly to me? When I was younger, I assumed that every slight or cross word was a direct criticism. Experience has taught me that I am just the recipient of someone else's anger or frustration. People do not wake up each morning plotting to make my life miserable. All people operate from a perspective of personal motive.

It is not someone else's job to make _my_ life nice.

When I am dissatisfied with conditions in my life, the temptation to blame or assign responsibility to others is a huge temptation. When I am not content with conditions surrounding me, it is _my_ job to analyze each situation and take action to make my life more pleasant. If I expect free will to make decisions, I have to accept that I am accountable for the outcome of those choices.

A parent is just a person who happens to be related to you.

Most people aim for perfection. The reality is we never achieve it. As a parent, I have done the best I can.

Be grateful for what I have been able to do to enrich your life, whether it is through actions or genetics! Try to forgive my human failings; I hope your children forgive yours.

A mother is a person who still has hopes and dreams.

I have been where you are, but you have never been where I am in life. Who I am on the inside is still that same woman who loves life.

My hopes and dreams are not static, but change as circumstances dictate. I am entitled to respect for my opinions, the joy I find in my life, and consideration for my physical limitations as I continue to grow older. Lessened physical capability does not equate with dementia!

Get over yourself!

Self-pity is crippling. Useless forays into "poor me" can be countered by helping others. My problems are minor compared to those of so many in the world who have much less than I do. When I "get out of myself" and run errands for a sick friend, join a community project, or listen to someone who just needs to connect, I develop a feeling of usefulness and purpose. I don't have time or energy to worry needlessly about my petty issues if my mind is filled with a constructive purpose.

I place my trust in God.

I look at the concept of a Supreme Being as a force known by many nicknames. By whatever name your Higher Power is called, this entity is the only one to display perfection. God, by working through others, possesses the power to help me navigate through the trials and joys of life. People are fallible; all will disappoint me at some time or another, but God is never too busy to listen to me and is always available to guide me.

If you can't say something in a pleasant voice, don't talk!

Sometimes, it's not what I'm saying, but how I'm saying it that causes misunderstandings. Conflict is a part of life. Nothing is accomplished if people feel attacked by me, or their feelings are intentionally wounded. I need to be honest, clear and kind in my style of communication with others. Disagreement does not require furious anger.

Fear is the root cause of all my anger.

If I am afraid that I will not get what I want or might have to give up something important to me, I become uncomfortable and feel that I am losing control of a situation. These fears produce anger that can take many forms: feeling uncomfortable, annoyance, frustration, agitation, verbal anger, rage, and meltdown! I need to set anger aside and put a name to my fear. By putting my focus on the specific fear, I can increase my chances of a solution.

Just because *I* don't know the answer doesn't mean there isn't an answer.

When I was younger, I thought I had to be emotionally self-sufficient. If I couldn't find a solution to a problem, I deemed it unsolvable. Today I try to be smart enough to ask for help when I reach a sticking point. The trick is to ask someone who has already experienced this same dilemma and survived with dignity and grace.

Sometimes when I am wandering around in my own head I am in questionable territory.

Most of us, including myself, have difficulty considering options that we do not want to contemplate. Instead, we cling to our own thought patterns. A trusted friend can be an objective observer who can become a valuable asset by pointing out options that I might not have addressed.

To be a happy person, I had to move from the childish position of "taker" to the adult position of "giver."

It's easy to spot the transformation of child to adult by watching children mature from a self-centered attitude of "me first" to one of recognition of the needs of others. When I am too much alone in my own thoughts, loneliness and self-centeredness creep in.

The solution is to "get over myself" and find someone to help.

I start and end my day with a connection to God.

I say a short prayer, thanking God for everything and everyone in my life. Gratitude moves me from a feeling of unrest to knowledge that I can depend on my Higher Power. God has become my safety net. Talking to God on a regular basis ensures that I remember my limitations, but need not feel alone.

I need to tell the people I love
that I care about them.

Sometimes actions are not enough; people need to hear the words. Voicing my love is never a wasted action. Once that person is no longer there, thinking about what I should have said is a poor substitute for not taking the time to connect.

Appreciate blessings.

Sometimes it is easy to take my gifts for granted. When I was born, the only choice I made was whether to live or die. Every other circumstance was out of my control. I did not choose my parents, health, intelligence, appearance, race, gender, nationality, talents, economic or social circumstances, siblings, or environment. If I look for the positive, I will realize that I was blessed!

Life is not fair; however, it can be wonderful!

Every day is an adventure! My task in life is to construct the best circumstances I can for myself given my set of life conditions. I have found it pointless to focus on problems; I need to discover solutions. Fairness comes as the result of working to improve my life and do the right thing.

Mistakes are a valuable part of learning.

I have learned more from my mistakes than successes. If I am to enjoy free will, I must accept that I (and others) will make mistakes. A person who makes no errors is not fully involved in life. Every experience I have molds me into the individual I am today. When someone does something to irritate me or makes a mistake, I remind myself, "It's not like I haven't done that." Everyone's mistakes are never a wasted effort if I learn from them!

All experiences are opportunities to grow.

I can view every circumstance as a problem **or** just one of life's opportunities to grow in understanding. I am a composite of everything that has happened in my life. Everyone I encounter is my teacher. If I view my enemies as resources, I can capitalize on those experiences. Lessons learned don't have to be repeated!

Everyone needs to know that family and friends care.

When I am too busy to connect with family or a friend, I am ignoring their need and focusing solely on myself. When I am lonely, my solution is to call someone and bring joy into his or her life. (They will welcome the call if I am not whining!)

Every day is a gift . . . cherish it.

I have known individuals who assumed they would have many years to heal arguments or correct stressful relationships. Make time today to take a loved one on vacation, to visit or call a relative or friend, or to let someone know how much they mean to you. All of those intentions can be rendered meaningless in an instant. Get busy and do it! Life happens.

Mothers really do remember what it was like to be your age!

I remember what it was like to be a teenager . . . I was smart and my parents were utterly clueless . . . (or so I thought). I remember the years of college, my children's issues, juggling family and work responsibilities, children leaving home, loneliness, and recreating my life after my children had lives of their own. I am a resource . . . don't waste it!

People are not mind readers.

If you want to matter to people, let them know they matter to you. Subtlety is lost on most of us. We need tangible proof demonstrated by words and deeds to see that someone cares. Speak up . . . hopefully with tact!

Trust is not an entitlement; it is earned.

I try to be an integrated person; ***my thoughts, words, and actions need to match.*** I only trust people who are honest about what they think and feel and show it by their words and behavior. Inconsistencies are easy to spot. Sometimes people can verbalize a polite response, but their eyes and face betray their inner thoughts. If I want to be considered a trusted friend, I must prove that I have no hidden agendas or intolerance.

I have a right to my opinion; however, I am not entitled to be rude.

Time and experience have taught me that I can get my point across best by eliminating the angry word "you . . ." from verbal exchanges. When I talk in a calm manner about **_my_** thoughts, feelings, beliefs and expectations, I do not launch the "steel ear lappers" that clang down over your ears.

People are not required to share my beliefs.

I am free to state my preferences because I live in a country where that is my right. Others also have the same right even if I think they are misinformed! That is the true beauty of living in our democracy. Tolerance for others and their opinions and ideas is the cornerstone for true communication.

Every person has value and deserves my respect.

It is true that how we treat others is how they respond to us. If I convey genuine respect for other cultures, religions, political issues, and social values, I have a greater chance of demonstrating tolerance and reducing friction. Our country resembles a recipe of a delicious cookie with lots of different ingredients. I am only one component.

Variety enriches my life.

Multi-faceted people are the defining ingredient in the quality of my friendships. Age, gender, ethnicity, and talents add spice to everyday living. If I only associate with others just like me, I cheat myself of the richness of diversity.

Life is going to have ups and downs . . . misery is optional.

When I am upset, I need to remember that I have options. Emotions prevent objectivity . . . I try to look at facts. Not all of my choices are going to be fun, but all of my options can be learning tools. When I focus on the negative, misery is the result. If I focus on the positives, I can view each event as a learning exercise. Tears are normal, but tears are not a solution.

Necessities are not the same as luxuries.

Necessities include food, shelter, clothing, health, and safety. Anything beyond that is what I term a luxury problem. I try to remember that most of those difficulties I am fretting about are just luxuries. Who wouldn't want a really nice house, fancy car, spectacular shoes, etc.? I must remember to count my blessings and acknowledge that most of what I value has to do with relationships, not "stuff."

Be kind to your parents.

Parents have feelings just like every other person. They need to know they are loved, appreciated, and valued. No one has perfect parents; they do the best they can, loving you even when you annoy them (which is often). My dad used to tease me that _he_ became considerably more intelligent once _I_ had reached the age of twenty-five. It is amazing how age and experience alter perspective!

Use one set of manners.

Every person is entitled to my best manners, regardless of social standing, bank account, age, gender, or ethnicity. If I expect others to treat me with politeness, I owe that same attitude to everyone I meet regardless of my mood. If I am having a difficult day, I am ***not*** entitled to spread the misery. When I am having a good day, I ***am*** obligated to share it.

Strive to keep a balanced perspective.

Every day offers its successes and disappointments. If I focus solely on what disturbs me, I allow that difficulty to crowd out a balanced perspective of the positives at that moment. I will not be consumed by negatives (such as bills and family problems) if I take the opportunity to remind myself about my many blessings. It also helps me to remind myself that when my car acts up, it does not mean that I will need a new motor . . . maybe it's just condensation in the fuel line!

Take a few minutes each day
to simply enjoy life.

I build time for reading, music, and conversations with friends into my daily routine. All my chores and responsibilities seem less odious when I have set aside time to relish the activities I hold dear. Everybody needs rewards!

God's plan is always better than my plan.

If I had been limited to what **I** planned for my life, I would have missed out on a lot of wonderful adventures. What seemed like a failure of my plan was, in reality, the substitution of something better. Hindsight reveals this. If my plans do not materialize, I am reassured that something better is in the works!

Character is the result of doing what is right, not what is easily accomplished.

When I do nothing about an injustice, I become part of the problem. Many people have given me assistance with my difficulties over the years. I need to remember that it was not always easy for them to accomplish this, nor was it always convenient. I can honor their actions by continuing their efforts to help others and do what is right.

Grandmothers and grandfathers are living history books.

My grandmother witnessed a span of history that encompassed ninety years. My mother was born at home in the winter and my grandfather went to fetch the doctor in a sleigh. There were so few cars in the state of Vermont in the early 1900's that the state published a list of license numbers and who owned them. This same grandmother witnessed World War I, The Great Depression, World War II, The Korean War, Viet Nam, the beginning of space flight, and the birth of technology. She knew how to cook from scratch and her meringue was two inches high on a lemon pie she made from basic ingredients. She did not use a mixer, just a wire whip. She was loyal to a fault and made the best of every situation. My father's mother came to this country as an immigrant, learned to speak English and bake extraordinary bread. Take time to preserve their stories. Don't waste their efforts to enlarge your education!

Travel! Open your mind to a new understanding.

Absolutely nothing gave me a better perspective about an area or country than actually being there. We are sensory creatures. The sounds, smells, tastes, and feel of the air and salt water cannot be duplicated in a video. Nothing has made me appreciate my country and its splendors more than comparison with others who share a different experience.

Other people do not control
my happiness.

Sometimes I fall into the trap of thinking that what other people say or do determines whether or not I have a happy day. Not so! It does not matter whether someone else is pleased or displeased with what I am thinking or doing . . . it really boils down to whether or not I am doing the right thing.

The principal aim of a parent is to raise an independent child.

I know that I have done my job if my adult children are able to express their beliefs, take care of their families, and are relatively happy with their relationships in their lives. Part of that task is to demonstrate love by telling my children what they **_need_** to hear including what they would rather not consider.

We all fall short of perfection.
(Even you!)

I recognize that just as I cannot achieve perfection, neither can my children . . . nor should I expect it! It's easier to be tolerant of my grandchildren's behavior because I have gained some perspective about what is genuinely important. I don't care now if they jump on the sofa, but heaven help my kids if they had tried it!

Life has softened my perspective.

I was a young mother. I felt it was important for my kids to have impeccable manners. I tried to impress the idea on my oldest son that it was important to assist me with my chair. When we were traveling, we stopped at our favorite diner. My five-year-old son dutifully got up to assist me with my chair. As he noticeably struggled to get the chair closer to the table, he muttered, "Mom, you sure have gained weight!" Two police officers sitting at the counter nearby started choking on their coffee, but to their credit, I didn't hear one snicker! We worked on the weight comments later.

It's ok to plan: just don't be surprised if that plan doesn't work or turns in a different direction.

I used to think that if I made a good plan, whether concerning my family, finances, or life goals . . . it was bound to work. Life has taught me to go with the flow. If my plan doesn't work . . . it will be adjusted or replaced by a better one. I just have to be patient and see what develops.

The happiest people I know focus on the positive.

If I am truthful, I can identify positive elements in **_every_** situation and relationship. I try to keep my focus on what is pleasant in my life. We all experience negatives in relationships, jobs, and everyday interactions with others. If I constantly rehash those negatives, they destroy all the beauty and joy in my life. To focus on the humor in every situation is a gift!

Whatever thought I focus on is a _**choice**_.

I can't always control what thought enters my mind, but I can control how long it stays! Worrying is different than looking for a solution. If I allow negative thoughts to linger, my mood deteriorates to one of despair or self-pity. Neither of those attitudes is constructive. It's like standing there fussing because the faucet is leaking all over the kitchen counter. I can fuss (worry), or I can turn the water off and do the repair (solution).

Forgive everybody!

At some point in my life I learned that holding resentments against others hurts **_me_**. Most people do the best they can. They are fallible, as am I. I find that I need to say to myself, "It's not like I haven't done it (or something similar)!" I need to focus on making improvements in my own behavior, not the behavior of others.

Life is not a level playing field, but I can offer assistance to those who want help.

I have an obligation to help others who need a hand up. Not everyone is born into a family possessing great intelligence, education, social skills, or wealth. I can always find someone who needs my help if I bother to look. I can show my gratitude for the life I've been given by helping others less fortunate.

Mistakes are the building blocks for better judgment.

Cherish your mistakes. Evaluate your mistakes. Learn from your mistakes. Do NOT ignore them. If I've tried something over and over and it still produces the same unsatisfactory result, it's time to take a clear look at ___why___ I am doing that particular behavior.

Any negative character traits
I possess are tied to a fear.

Character traits can be neutral, positive, or negative. When something triggers one of my fears, the temptation is to protect myself. For example: If I am afraid that someone will not think of me in a good light, I am tempted to embellish certain facts, or omit negative information because I am afraid I will not measure up. The solution is to address my fear. If my fear is unreasonable, I ignore it. However, if it is a valid fear I focus on what is in my control to effect a change in me.

My courage comes from faith in God.

I am just one small being in this great universe. Yet every time I look to God to help me find answers or weave my way through a difficult situation, the answer is provided. This is contingent upon my willingness to open my mind to new directions. When I stubbornly cling to old ideas, I am blind to inspiration. I believe that God provides answers through other people if I am open to suggestions.

People are the greatest gift in life.

Everyone is my teacher. Through them I have learned how to love, how to obtain happiness, and how to deal with loss. From discontented people I have learned how to avoid being crabby. From happy people full of appreciation for life, I have learned how to experience joy. From people who have weathered the storms of life, I have learned how to rely on God and the goodness of most humans.

Unconditional love is my goal.

If I only care about someone when they are doing what I want, saying what I want to hear, and paying attention to me, then I am engaging in self-centered love. All humans disappoint those who care about them; if I truly love someone, I accept them in spite of differences and failure to meet my sometimes excessive expectations.

Tears are not a solution.

Tears are sometimes a welcome release from sadness or worry. That is all they are. Crying never fixes my problems or heals emotional hurts. Relief comes from identifying what I am afraid of and taking steps to heal my hurts.

Self-pity prevents me from looking at a situation honestly.

I am fortunate to have good friends who tell me to "get over myself" when I sink into despair. When I adopt the mind-set of "poor me" I am incapable of taking an objective view of any situation. I strive to balance the negative with all the positives in my life.

Make everyone who matters to you feel important.

Every person, regardless of age, longs to have some recognition that they are special. Whether a relative or friend, everyone wants to be uniquely connected to others.

The people I trust are the individuals who tell me the truth . . . what I need to hear, not what I want to hear.

Reality (objectivity) is difficult to process, especially if it is not what I would enjoy. Friends, who try to spare my feelings instead of talking candidly, inadvertently deny me knowledge that improves my decision-making ability. The answer to any dilemma must begin with the truth.

I can't help anyone who does not want help.

It is distressing to watch people I care about immerse themselves in chaos; anything I say will fall upon deaf ears if an individual is unwilling to consider counsel. I am not a hammer; they are not a nail! All I can do is let them know I am available if they want to talk.

People cannot read my mind.

I need to be clear when communicating with others. I need to let them know if I am looking for a solution, or if I just want to vent. Few experiences are as frustrating as listening to someone rage on and on about a problem, then refusing all suggestions for a solution. If I am the person attempting to transfer my angst to them, I must recognize that it will not result in a solution. If I am looking for answers, I need to do more listening than talking.

Life happens, whether it's
convenient or not.

Sometimes I have excellent plans. But, in spite of my best efforts, life intervenes and scuttles them. Problems are seldom convenient! Experience has taught me that there are many scenarios that are beyond my control . . . health, the stock market, the economy, and family emergencies. All of these have, at one time or other, compelled me to change direction. And it has all worked out when I apply myself to a better solution!

Do not blame your parents for situations in your adult life that distress you.

The quality of anyone's life is dependent upon acquiring the ability to deal with disappointment, loss, frustration, and everyday life decisions. Parents do the best they can. Everyone arrives in adulthood with some baggage. (Your parents did too!) Assigning blame is not a solution. If I am unhappy, it is not because my parents failed me; it is the consequence of my lack of skill in developing abilities to cope with situations and personalities that cause me distress. As an adult I can learn constructive remedies for anything that troubles me!

Enjoy maturity!

The lack of ageing is death. Every birthday is an accomplishment. If I lived 150 years ago, I would not have the benefit of personal freedoms, health cures, or opportunities afforded to women in the present day. My grandmothers were restricted by lack of opportunity, education, technology, and medical science. I have every expectation of living a full, useful, and rewarding existence far into my senior years. What a gift!

Stand up for those who need help.

If I am not part of the solution to a situation, then I must recognize that I continue to support the problem. Injustice does not simply disappear . . . it must be corrected. I try to remember those individuals who gave me a helping hand when I was in the midst of mayhem. The feeling that I was not alone and their actions on my behalf carried me through whatever chaos invaded my life.

I can't _**make**_ anyone do anything.

I am not in control of the behavior of _**other**_ people. I am, however, in control of _**my**_ own thoughts and actions. I can only change how _**I**_ behave toward others and respond to their actions or indifference.

Forgive everybody.

People do the best they can. They do not get up
in the morning plotting how to make my life
miserable. No matter what the offense is, I have
probably done something similar to them or
someone else. Pointing fingers is not a solution.
Grant others compassion when they are wrong
and be grateful that you are not the person who
must be humble and seek forgiveness.

"No" is not a dirty word.

Everyone needs boundaries. Children feel safest when they have a clear picture of what is permitted. Parents are required to furnish food, shelter, clothing, and nurturing; extras are not entitlements. When kids do not associate responsibilities with privileges, they assume that they can receive whatever they ask for. This cheats them of the experience of anticipation.

Grow up every day.

People who appreciate life are involved in life on a daily basis. The most interesting people I know strive every day to be a more valuable person, a better friend, and a more effective member of the community. The challenges I encounter while interacting with people make me feel alive and teach me how to handle sticky situations with poise and grace.

Enjoy life!

All lives are a balance of joy and disappointment; that is the nature of our human experience. Take time to pursue a favorite activity, appreciate nature, travel, and spend time with friends. Life passes in a heartbeat; don't let a moment go by that is not appreciated!

Keep in touch.

The easiest excuse in the world for not calling someone up is the idea of lack of time. Everyone is busy. The reality is that we ***make time*** for people who are important to us. It's too late to change what I did yesterday. I need to call people today; there are no guarantees for tomorrow.

Wish, plan, action!

I can wish and plan for a long time, but action is what creates a change. Until I take the final step of action, all my plans are just dreams.

A parent's job is guidance . . .
not continual rescue or prevention.

It is natural for me to assume that I have some stake in my child's actions. However, my job as a parent is to lend support and counsel, not fix the problem. When I take over, I deprive my child of the experience of understanding that choices have consequences. I have always learned just as much from my errors as from success.

Children are not mind readers; talk to them about your views of the world.

Children pretend not to hear your ideas. It is natural for teens to discount what you say. Say it anyway. If you listen closely, I guarantee that you will hear your thoughts exit their mouths when they are talking to their friends!

It is easier to stop harsh words spilling from my mouth than to do damage control after they have escaped.

I can hear my mother cautioning me, "If you can't say something pleasant, don't utter a word." Nobody wants to listen to a tirade of emotions. The years have taught me that calm objectivity is welcome in stressful situations. I always have to remember the goal of the conversation, not my frustration with the issue.

I can never go back;
there are no do-overs.

Continual regret is a waste of time. I need to take an objective view of the memory, assess my part in the action, and learn from my errors. When I make a conscious effort to do this, I prevent similar mistakes in the present and in the future.

Parents who love their children are never disappointed *in* them; they are disappointed *for* them.

Genuine love is unconditional. It allows me to accept people as they are, not how I want them to be. As a parent, I only want what is best for my children. Mistakes are a valuable part of the learning process. When I am grinding my teeth over drama involving my family, I try to remember that each of us has a path to follow, and 'potholes' are a predictable occurrence. Children will learn valuable information about themselves from mistakes *if* they take time to analyze what went wrong. My love for them does not diminish because they commit errors.

Forgive everyone . . .
trust is another matter.

It is silly for me to focus on judgment of others. Everyone does things that hurt or annoy others. The real problem is trust. Can I, or should I, trust some individuals when they hurt me. Forgiveness is easily given; trust, once broken, must be earned again.

Make it a practice to do the right thing.

The only entity I need to be concerned about pleasing is God. Humans are always fallible. They have personal agendas, ideas, and aspirations. I try to do the right thing according to the values I have been taught or acquired (even if it causes conflict) rather than take the least stressful course of action.

Integrity is the ultimate goal.

Others perceive my character based on what I do . . . not just what I say. We all have grand ideas, but it is performance that counts. An integrated person thinks, acts, and speaks with one voice. There should be no confusion when people assess my character.

Life itself is not based on fairness;
it is my job to help promote this.

No child chooses where birth occurs. Nor does the child have a say in choosing its parents, race, health, intelligence, appearance, or culture. It is up to me to make the most of my opportunities. It is also a given that I should help those who need assistance. I show my gratitude for the gifts I have been given by helping others.

"Because I said so," is a valid response.

Kids only feel safe when someone is in charge . . . preferably not them. It is unreasonable for me to expect a teenager to possess the wisdom of an adult. They have not had the same experiences that I have undergone, not do they possess the wisdom that was generated from those 'adventures'. There is no substitute for actual life experiences. Kids are unable to see past the feeling that they are 'bulletproof' and get themselves in complicated situations. Doing a satisfactory job as a parent does not depend on my children's approval; it is based on guidance.

Conflict is inevitable.
Respect is mandatory.

It is unreasonable to expect that all my children and acquaintances will be happy with my choices and beliefs. I define conflict as a difference of opinion. I am entitled to my opinion, just as you have the right to yours. When that difference of opinion is handled with respect, we can deal with the issues and not succumb to an emotional tug of war. Differences are what make us interesting. If I want others to respect my point of view, I must do the same for them. Think how boring it would be if everyone thought and acted the same!

Make a point to call people.

Nobody wants to hear that the reason you have not called is, "I was busy" or "I forgot." Translated, that means that they were not important enough to create a contact. Everyone is busy. Everyone has obligations. Our human contacts are the most precious gift we have been given. Don't waste them.

Put time and effort into your relationships.

When someone I care about says that they didn't call me because they were too busy, I can't help but wonder if I am really important to them. Everybody is busy. Time given to others has more importance than money . . . spend it wisely.

Hair is irritating;
be glad you have some!

When I look at what I **have** instead of what I lack, I can be grateful for the important things in life—health, adequate shelter, food, and other necessities. Much of the world's population lacks basic necessities or even the ability to improve their lot in life.

Be grateful you are growing older.

Consider this: The only alternative to ageing is death! From the moment we are born, we are moving toward the inevitable conclusion of life. Growing older, however, is not the end of an interesting existence. At every stage of my life I have been required to adjust my activities to accommodate my physical capabilities. Like everything else in life, a quality experience requires effort. There is a life rich in possibilities waiting just for you. Explore your options.

Be grateful for becoming wiser.

Wisdom is simply learning how to avoid the everyday pitfalls that confront me on a regular basis. Someone once told me that if I was suffering, stop doing what I did to get in that predicament! Misery teaches me that if I don't want to continue to be unhappy, I must change what I am doing. I am not required to repeat past mistakes if I learn how to function differently. Introspection is seldom fun, but it is necessary for growth.

Death comes to everyone.

From the moment I was born I was slated to die. As uncomfortable as this subject is, it needs consideration. As a child, I remember thinking that death was for other people who were really ancient, had lots of wrinkles, and didn't want to live anymore. Reality intruded when young acquaintances passed away. In adulthood I came to understand that being careful does not necessarily guarantee a long life. Fate is unpredictable. My task is to <u>live</u> my life . . . not just exist. Don't get bogged down in tedium. Appreciate the time you have been given.

Do you want your life to be an adventure or an endurance contest?

You choose! It's as simple as that. Everyone has obligations . . . work, childcare, cleaning chores, laundry, bills to be paid, and appointments to keep. A balanced life includes joy. Perspective is the deciding factor. Simple pleasures can be derived from the most ordinary sources. Music, art, sports, gardening, pets, community projects, helping others, and meeting people outside your normal experience all contribute to a satisfying existence.

Reality check: Gravity always wins in the end.

The time I waste worrying about wrinkles, sags, or a few added pounds would be better spent occupying my mind with constructive endeavors. Stunning visual appeal or youth does not guarantee happiness. I've never seen an epitaph that proclaimed that the person was stunning or had huge muscles. We are remembered (despite our wrinkles or weight) for what we contribute to others.

Love is an action word.

When a person truly loves someone, they show that love through their behavior. Intentions are not actions. If a person never hears from you or feels ignored because you are too busy, they feel as though they don't matter to you.

I am not responsible for another person's mistakes.

Because I care about the people I love, I sometimes fall into the trap of thinking that I should have done something to prevent their mistakes. I might better spend my energy figuring out how to prevent my own missteps. That is certainly a better use of my time!

Relationships are fragile.

I don't need to complicate them with selective honesty or wishing that someone would change to suit me. If I make it a practice to consistently treat someone with compassion, trust, and respect, I lessen the chance that I will create a rift in a relationship that leads to its destruction.

Appreciate your heritage.

My great-grandparents never saw a cell phone or a computer or traveled in an airplane. They worked tirelessly to provide a better life for their families. Some were immigrants who were required to learn a new language in order to fit themselves into a new culture. One was a single parent who sold corsets door to door. They died before I became an adult and never had the opportunity to see the results of all their efforts to improve the life that is available to me. I remain forever grateful for their contributions to my attitudes toward living.

Nobody reaches perfection; that does not mean I shouldn't try to improve the way I deal with my daily life.

Happiness is not a separate entity. It arrives as a result of consistently trying to put forth a better effort each and every day to improve my relationships with others, help someone else, meet my responsibilities, and do the next right thing. The recipe is easy; it's the <u>doing</u> that requires exertion.

Our wisdom is the most valuable legacy we leave to our children.

Subtlety is often lost on others. Our voices will live on if our children hear what we believe combined with an explanation of why we choose a value. Demonstrating our beliefs is the ultimate expression.

I do not always get the opportunity to choose.

I have no control over who dies or leaves my life. People get older, friends and relatives move, world events impact my life, ill health happens, and those I love depart this life. In response, I **can** choose to value those I love, let them know I care, visit people I miss, experience all I can of what life has to offer, and adjust to the different requirements of my place on the continuum of life. I would like to reflect on my experiences and know that something I did mattered to those I love. I choose only my own behavior.

If I am not actively seeking a solution, I am still part of the problem.

Maturity has taught me that I can complain, whine, drip copious amounts of tears, blame others, and continually fuss about something that bothers me, **BUT** those actions will not make the issue go away. I only achieve relief when I begin to search out solutions and take action.

Revitalize your enthusiasm for life.

Stress is a great destroyer of contentment and hope. It is necessary for me to periodically take stock of how I am spending my time. I try to always remember to balance responsibility with nurturing my zest for living. The time I invest in doing something pleasurable renews my gusto for enjoying daily activities.

You don't have to agree with anything I have said or written.

If you would rather do it your way, you can reinvent the wheel, blunder through the same dramas I did, and take your lumps. Experience and pain are very effective instructors. Remember, I love you anyway!

ADDITIONAL REMINDERS

_____

_____

_____

_____

_____

_____

_____

_____

_____

_____

_____

_____

_____

_____

_____

_____

_____

_____

_____

_____

_____

_____

_____

_____

ADDITIONAL REMINDERS

_____

_____

_____

_____

_____

_____

_____

_____

_____

_____

_____

_____

_____

_____

_____

_____

_____

_____

_____

_____

_____

_____

ADDITIONAL REMINDERS

_____
_____
_____
_____
_____
_____
_____
_____
_____
_____
_____
_____
_____
_____
_____
_____
_____
_____
_____
_____
_____
_____
_____
_____

ADDITIONAL REMINDERS

_____
_____
_____
_____
_____
_____
_____
_____
_____
_____
_____
_____
_____
_____
_____
_____
_____
_____
_____
_____
_____
_____
_____
_____
_____
_____
_____

ADDITIONAL REMINDERS

_____
_____
_____
_____
_____
_____
_____
_____
_____
_____
_____
_____
_____
_____
_____
_____
_____
_____
_____
_____
_____
_____
_____
_____
_____
_____